GREYLAND YOUTH ORGANIZATION

Published by:
Dreamcatchers, and The literary division of
Greyland Youth Organization

ISBN -13: 978-0615896236
ISBN-10: 0615896235

Printed in the United States of America
Edited by RCC Muse Literary Staff Members:
Jo Scott-Coe MFA– Mark Anthony Howard – Maribel Banuelos
And Cynthia L. Castaneda

Third Edition

The ABC's of a Black Man's Principles

Table of Contents

Foreword

I want to write something significant. I don't want to be popular... I want to be profound. This is my submission of my perspective to the world. Malcolm said self sufficient, the Nation of Islam shot him and we forgot. May I be blessed of God to resume Malcolm's marathon. Moses led Israel from bondage and into the wilderness. Joshua succeeded him and led Israel into the promise land. In promise of their own promised land, would Black people leave Egypt on their own free will? I just want to offer the option, the option for our own perspective and our own objective. What happened to the Negro League after Jacky Robinson's integration into the Major League Baseball? It was gradually dissolved and discontinued. With the contentment of integration, the option for Blacks to exist independent in America has died. This is my attempt at its revival.

I believe there should be a singular establishment to umbrella a collective group that is considerate to the *current* state of Black, but in leadership towards the *future* of Black. I believe that we should be educating our Black youth to be self sustaining; primarily through the growth and development of Black business communities and secondarily through Black residential communities. The concentration of Black agenda should be shifted towards the future of Black, its sustenance, and its direction. It is sad and shameful to see how blind and misguided we are as a collective people. It is sad to see the knowledge of ourselves as a people and our long-term progressive growth superseded by such trivial ignorance, division, contentment, and short-term selfishness.

There is no concurrent Black agenda. There is no delegated Black leadership. There is no Black leadership encouraging Black independence. There is no leader encouraging self sufficiency. There is no leader encouraging Black enterprise and there is no whisper of any Black Nationalism. Black people have become content with its assumed equal integration into American. There is no struggle. There is no agenda. There is no objective. There is no revolution. There is no Martin and there is no Malcolm.

I'm a humble Young black man named Mark Anthony Howard with a provocative ideal to pick up where the Black community let Martin and Malcolm die. It is my ideal to lead Black people away from the luxuries of Egypt as Moses did, back into the wilderness, and into the direction of our own promised land. This is my initiating submission to the world for a Black American objective of complete self sufficiency and independence. This is my submission of a foundation that I may build

6

upon that ideal. This my subtle stir of the settled Black Nationalism. This is my contribution to America and the Black American Community. This is my contribution toward the enrichment of a Young Black American Future.

The paradise hope of Moses' is still attainable for God's people, but we have to assume being Black as a responsibility and not as an excuse. We are the most struggled people of all time. I believe this should be a truth in our identity, but we tend to forget why and even that, we are struggling. We tend to forget our purpose. I believe that we may have forgotten our objective. We are such a fun, and high spirited people that we learn to enjoy what is now — despite any oppression or adversity. But, in order to reach an actual equality for our following generations we must take better accountability for ourselves and attach a deeper, further reaching purpose to our struggle. This book and its contents are my initiating steps toward the enrichment of that purpose.

Introduction

P is for Principles! A principle is guiding sense of the requirements and obligations of rightful conduct. A principle is a rule, a code, a law, a standard, a theory, and a belief. A principle is the fundamental foundation of reasoning. The principled man has resolved to govern his conduct in accordance with his dogma.

I believe that principle is the essential element that Black men may be missing, and need to develop into a successful people as a whole, or at the least to begin in direction towards that goal. I believe we all know of the patches in our community that are left un-whole by broken homes absent of the father. This is a terrible occurrence that we have become accustom to as Black people. I believe that our faults, shortcomings, and ignorance as a Black people are completely stemmed to this. The aftermath and repercussion (especially for Black men) is that we lack the foundational teachings and principles that our White, Latino, and Asian brothers are *lovingly* taught by their direct examples (their fathers) of those teachings.

I have heard black leadership quarrel of the term disenfranchised in regards to or in reference to Black people. I have taken it upon myself to become educated of the term and I recently learned the full meaning for the word disenfranchised and what it details. In relative terms to business, disenfranchise is to deprive of some privilege or right.

With that definition I believe that any child that has not been taught by a loving man, the principles of how to be a man, has been deprived of what should be a fundamental right to guidance. So with this book I offer, to the ever growing population of young Black men who have been disenfranchised, *my own* standard of principles, I believe, a Black man should have looked to base himself around. These are just the fundamental definitions that I believe can, and should, be developed upon further in a personalization within each young man.

This short book was meant simply as an introduction to these essential principles. As each young man matures – the meanings, definitions, and applications should become wider, deeper, stronger, and fuller. I believe these fundamental principles, when practiced, could change the state of Black as a whole. A basic architectural principle conveys that you cannot build anything sound, and withstanding, without a strong foundation. I like to somehow start mandating these principles and their perspective as the standard foundation for Young Black men— in the collective build of the next generation of Black men.

9

The ABC's of a Black Man's Principles

I'd like the next generation of Black men to be the architectural design of a conscious group of today's Black men. A lot of work is needed in the rehabilitation of the Black community and I'd like to initiate the force by swinging the first axe or figurative hammer.

"We're always talking about how broken Black men are, but perhaps we should be focused on the rebuilding rather than the demolition. The media is with the demolition crew. But as a Black community, we need to be with the architects and the builders. It's really up to us as a community to unite and build our Black men up regardless of what's in the media." ~ Raquel Gordon

The ABC's

Of

A Black Man's Principles

Chapter One

ABC

The ABC's of a Black Man's Principles

"I will not excuse or offer justifications for my actions that are in accordance with the person I am."-Mark Anthony Howard

Ais for Accountability - Within an organization, the principles and practices of ethical accountability aim to improve both the internal standard of individual and group conduct. Accountability is the absolute A in the ABC's of principles. Accountability is the alpha principle necessary to grow progressively toward a successful people as a whole. As Black men learn to grow in their principles, particularly in their willingness to accountability — we grow in willingness to accept a complete responsibility for ourselves, our past, our current, and most importantly our future. As we learn to grow accountable we fully accept the responsibilities necessary in progressing ourselves as a people for the next generation.

I think the importance in the principle of accountability extends itself further than just conduct. It is also relative in external factors, such as sustainable economic and ecologic **strategy**. These strategies are an absolute necessity in order to build any type of self-sustaining structure such as the type needed in a new Black culture. A growth is needed in the Black community and there can be no growth without accountability.

"Like Christ said, love thee one another. I learned to do that, and I learned to respect and be appreciative and thankful for what I had." – James Brown

A is for Appreciative – Appreciative is an adjective basically defined to be thankful, grateful, and indebted for, or towards, someone or something. It is also defined as having or showing appreciation. An appreciative person recognizes value and therefore enables its increase. That is what appreciation is in fact; the recognition of aesthetic value and that value's increase.

You have to be an appreciative person in life. You have to recognize the value that God and other people may be adding to you. Nothing is worse than an ungrateful person. Nothing is worse than adding value to someone who does not recognize, acknowledge, or appreciate it.

We all come into a world with nothing. From that moment each of our life's acquisitions and necessities are filled by contributions from others. As infants and children we should be entitled (certainly not a guarantee) to a certain amount of provisions. But as mature teens and adult men we should appreciate that nothing is owed to us. From then we should learn to show and have an appreciation to all the things that God and others may have willingly added, or be adding, to our value.

The most valued man is an appreciative man, because an appreciative man knows the most value. Appreciation is very good.

"We have to dare to be ourselves, however frightening or strange that self may prove to be."
–May Sarton

A is for Authenticity - To be authentic is to be of undisputed truth, factual origin, and to be genuine. Authenticity also refers to the truthfulness of values, principles, commitments, attributions, sincerity, devotion, purpose, and intentions.

Because a man's authenticity is the credible weld his whole self— it should be his most valued and uncompromising attribute. The resiliency to maintain his apparent (or exclaimed) origin is the whole measurement of man's purity. It is relevant to the difference in gold being measured as 8 carat gold and 24 carat gold. Ask yourself are you an 8 carat man or a 24 carat man? From his internal— outward to his external — a man's factual consistency and genuine hardiness is the authentic measure of that man. Does that make sense? Let's go a little deeper for a moment.

In philosophy, the conscious self is seen as coming to terms with being in the material world and with encountering external forces, pressures, and influences which are very different from, and other than itself. (One more part) Authenticity is the measureable degree to which one is true to his own personality, spirit, or character despite these pressures. Got that? Pretty deep huh?

As the world happens to us and around us, its pressures may encourage a conform to uniformity. Authenticity is sort of an impenetrable cloak or defensive force field around a man's true identity, because it is his true identity. It's like his own self-generated and inward force. The more authentic the man — the stronger his cloaking force. (This is why I believe Ironman to be the best Marvel Hero. All others have some freak fusion of genes, while Ironman is a self generating force. To kill him you would have to kill his force. And to kill his force you would have to remove it, which would kill you. Haha! Ironman is undisputedly the most authentic Marvel hero.)

The ABC's of a Black Man's Principles

Authenticity is also the strongest personal principle of my own. In my personal outlook I have a hard time believing that I am born of any divine privilege, entitlement, or that I am destined to become any type of special significance based upon my own esteem or unique skills. What I do believe is that there are a lot of solid characteristics and principles that I have developed and based myself upon that make me an exceptional man. The greatest amongst these principles is my own authenticity. I truly believe that I am exactly who I exclaim to be. I believe so much in my own authenticity that I feel it excessive to exclaim aloud. It is simply my undisputed truth. Despite any of my life's circumstance, however justifiably compromising, I have proven to be all parts of pure, genuine, and truthful character. My authenticity is my proudest attribute and what I truly believe distinguishes me as an authoritative perspective, individual, and Black man.

I believe that as Black men exercise a conscious effort to develop within their own authenticity — they would consequently grow resilient to societal pit-falls and recognize resolutions to counter the negative connotations meant to discourage the progression of Black Men.

"Happiness is not a matter of intensity but of balance, order, rhyme and harmony."-Thomas Merton

B is for Balance- Balance is a word used in many different ways with many different definitions. Balance is defined as both a noun and a verb. As a noun, it can be described as a state of equilibrium or equipoise; equal distribution of weight, or amount. It also can be something used to produce equilibrium; a counterpoise.

As a verb, balance can be described to bring to or to hold in equilibrium; a poise. To arrange, adjust, or proportion the parts of symmetry to be equal. Balance is also used as an accounting term meaning to add up the two sides of (an account) and determine the difference so that the sums of the two sides will be equal.

The definition of balance I find most relevant is in its noun form, as a mental steadiness or emotional stability. Balance defined as a mental state is simply maintaining the habit of calm behavior and judgment.

This is such an essential definition in the principle of balance, because the combination of mental steadiness and emotional stability absolutely enables us of our best decisions. What I believe is that a balance perspective is what should be strived for. In a balanced perspective one is considerate of all things evenly, and able to make judgments and decisions in the most rationale fashion. Sometimes life demands our attention heavily in a particular direction such as a semester of school or a work project. With so much focus in one direction sometimes a person must come back and redistribute his or her attention on the things that he or she may have neglected during that time. A good balance enables a person to progress evenly at a perpetual pace. Balance is not only a great principle for Black men — I believe it is the most practical principle for an optimal life. A good balance is good!

The ABC's of a Black Man's Principles

"Character cannot be developed in ease and quiet. Only through experience of trial and suffering can the soul be strengthened, vision cleared, ambition inspired, and success achieved" –Helen Keller

---

C is for Character – Character is the mental, moral, and conducting qualities distinctive to an individual. To have character is a priceless possession. To have character is to have principles. To have character is to have integrity. A man of character is a man of genuine personality, quality, and characteristics. Having character is the most essential ingredient in the making of a well-rounded and genuine person. A man without character is an omelet with no egg. Does that make any sense? In today's world it does. In today's world it is more important to be a character, than to have any. Men today rather perfect their portrayal of a character (usually one they have seen on television or a movie), than develop their own and possess genuine character. Men today don't have character, they are characters. Men today have become simple actors, imitating their rendition of their favorite character. This is not the reflection of definitive character; this is in fact, the exact opposite!

I believe the diminishing distinction between having character and being a character is shameful. Movies and television were intended to be enjoyed as entertainment. Today's men have become so infatuated with pop entertainers, musicians, and actors that they have forgotten the essential ingredients in the making of themselves as genuine men. Developing character is not optional. A man that has forgotten to prioritize the importance of character in his own life cannot properly emphasize the importance of character in any youth.

It is sad to see young boys headed in no direction towards the development of any quality characteristics. Their only direction is in the mimic of characters they see on TV, magazines, and movies. It is even more disappointing to see old men perpetuating the same behavior, and imitating their own version of the same characters.

The development of character is not optional. Character as a principle is so very important that the title of this book could very fittingly be substituted as "The ABC's of A Black Man's Character!" Black men, and all men, should be prioritizing the development of character within themselves, and within the next generation's youth. And not imitating (acting) the characters (actors) that are presented for the purpose of entertainment.

Real life is not your favorite movie. Real life is not your favorite reality television show. Real life is real life and the development of quality character is essential to it. Movies and television are meant as entertaining imitations of life. A man's life should not be an entertaining imitation of movies and television. My entire point is, develop character not characters! Character is Great!

> "It's not what we do once in a while that shapes our
> lives. It's what we do consistently"
> – Anthony Robbins

C is for Consistency – Consistency is the condition of cohering or holding together and retaining form; a solidity or firmness. A consistency can also be a steadfast adherence to the same principles, course, or form!

Consistency is absolutely one of the most important principles of foundation you can have for your life. Not only should consistency be a major principle for Black Men, but it should be the core principle of a MAN. A man is only a man in his consistency. A man can be any type of man he chooses, but only if he proves himself consistent with that choice. In fact, I would be so forward as to say a man *is* his consistency. You only are what you do and prove to be consistently.

Chapter Two

DEF's

"Let discernment be your trustee and mistakes be
your teacher."- T. F. Hodge

Dis for **Discernment** - Discernment is the ability to make good judgments. This is a basic principle that is very easy to apply to everyday life. If you don't have the ability to make and use good judgment, your life can never maintain any positive progress, or purpose. I believe this to be a very essential and elementary principle in application to the build of anything; much more especially to the build of a man, the rebuild of the Black man, and his community. You have to have good judgment otherwise everything you do will be foolish. A good discernment is great principle for a man to carry.

"True freedom is impossible without a mind made free by discipline"–Mortimer J. Adler

Dis for Discipline - Discipline is the practice of teaching and enforcing acceptable patterns of behavior, and the ability to behave in a controlled and calm way, even in a difficult or stressful situation.

If a Black man ever needed to exercise a principle – discipline (control), is that principle. Discipline enables all of a man's character to actualize. Restraint, reserve, and control are such necessary characteristics for the trials of success. Every principle foundation that a young man could build himself upon will at some point be threatened, scrutinized, or criticized. Discipline is an exercise that allows a man to with-stand compromising himself, his principles, and ultimately his integrity. Discipline is good!

> "With the minimum of resources and the minimal of provisions, I can absolutely maximize myself and my opportunities. This is my efficiency."
> –Mark Anthony Howard.

E is for Efficiency - Efficiency is the ability to do something well or to achieve a desired result without wasted energy or effort. I think that this is a highly applicable principle in any person's life. Life is hard as it is. Efficiency becomes very important when you don't have the privilege or resource to do things inefficiently. We as Black men have to learn to do things the right way the first time. Times are becoming extremely hard and crucial for Black men. Young Black men especially need to learn that efficiency is the key to wealthy living and wealthy habits.

McDonalds serves about 68 million customers a day in 33,000 restaurants across 118 countries. If one hamburger is dropped in each store, each day for a month at $1.29 a burger, the company loses $42,570 a day and $1,277,100 for the month. You might think that's small change for a billion dollar company but that's exactly the point—small things matter! This is especially true on a large scale. Imagine if some inefficient employees just went nuts for a whole year and threw *two* hamburgers on the floor every day. That would add up to 30 million dollars in inefficiencies!

The point is that small inefficiencies add up on top of each other and can make a big difference in people's lives. Black men have to stop ignoring their inefficiencies as a whole and learn to make small changes toward becoming more efficient as people, business, and community.

Black people are considered major consumers in the retail world. We should start to consider ourselves as a high yielding company as well. In a nationwide consumer report, Black buyers spent over 1 billion dollars a year for the last decade as retail and online shoppers. That's 10 billion dollars in ten years. The shameful inefficiency of this is that all of these dollars are accounted as dollars spent outside of Black owned businesses. This is a terrible inefficiency.

American statistics report that 54 percent of Black marriages end in divorce. This is also inefficiency. If that is not a disappointing enough statistic, 71 percent of black children sleep in homes where there father is not present. These are shameful reflections of inefficiency. Again, I think it is imperatively urgent for Black men to stop ignoring our inefficiencies and learn to make changes toward becoming more efficient as a people, a business, and a conscious community.

27

The ABC's of a Black Man's Principles

"Education is our passport to the future, for tomorrow belongs to the people who prepare for it today."-Malcolm X

E **is for Education** - Education is the process of receiving or giving systematic instructions. In its general sense, education is a form of learning in which skills, knowledge, and habits of a group of people are transferred from one generation to the next, through teaching, training, experience, or research. There is no substitution for education. If you want to grow you have to know. If you want to know you have to learn. There is no shortcut around education. Through America's premier College systems, there are some very well educated young Black men in this country. It is they, who should be leading the way as a collective group of ideals, principles, and examples for others to follow.

I also believe that American College institutes should not be the only form of education available. My ideal is that American College educated Black's should also take the accountability for the relay of their education. I think that community education programs should be implemented and mandated to establish a higher standard of bottom line for our Black youth, adolescent, unemployed, and elderly communities.

28

The ABC's of a Black Man's Principles

There is no growth without education. It would be nice for every member of the Black community to attend some college but that would not be a realistic expectation. I would like to simply see the opportunity and the options available for Black community members to educate themselves through Black avenues, programs, and channels.

There should be more organizations aside from, but in addition to, churches who offer educational community programs. In my perspective, it is futile to forum in regards to any problem without ever offering, or intending towards, its resolution. The purpose of education is to develop one's mind to think critically and creatively in order to problem solve independently with a rational, systematic approach. I believe that purpose should be applied to the creative spreading of education throughout the Black community outside of, but also in addition to, American school systems. Public high school should not be the only mandate of education required in our Black community. It should be our own responsibility to disperse through our community a quality standard of education. A very simple proverb states: "If you don't know you can't grow." Education is great!

"...Count it all Joy when you fall into various trials, knowing that the testing of your faith produces patience. " - James 1:2

F is for Faith – Faith is a confident belief in the truth, value, or trustworthiness of a person, idea, or thing. Faith can also be a set of principles, ideals, or beliefs. A person's faith is an unshakeable belief in something especially without proof or evidence of it.

The Bible book of Hebrews is full of examples of men and women who were loved by God for their works of faith. Each one believed, trusted, and exercised faith in the word of God despite a vague understanding. My favorite lessons of faith are in the Bible book of James.

The bible book of James conveys that faith without works cannot be called faith at all. Faith must work, it must produce. It must be visible. A verbal faith is not enough and mental faith alone is insufficient. Faith must be there, but it must also be more. Faith must be more than a passive possession — it should be an aggressive expression.

True faith manifests itself under pressure and in trials, because trial is the true test of faith. A person's trials may come and go but a strong faith will face them head on and develop endurance. As Black men each of us may have to endure something trying. As we develop

individually into manhood these trials may even increase. A strong faith

in God, principles, and oneself will enable the confident mind and heart

each man may need to successfully endure through each of his trials.

Faith is so good and so essential in the life of each Black man. I pray for

yours.

"Winning requires reaching inside of yourself for
that extra gear to accelerate through challenges."
- Orrin Woodward

F is for Fortitude - Fortitude is the strength of mind that enables a person to encounter danger or bear pain and/or adversity with courage. Fortitude is an essential principle for a Black man to build upon. There are so many adversities to progress. Anything a man can achieve for himself or for his identity is going to be contested at some point, in some way. I encourage each man to develop his fortitude and attack those opposing obstacles fervently.

Chapter Three

GHI's

"There is no better teacher than adversity. Every defeat, every heartbreak, every loss, contains its own seed, its own lesson on how to improve your performance next time." – Malcolm X

G is for Grit - Grit is a firmness of character. Grit is defined as a perseverance and passion for long term goals. Grit is conceptualized as a stable trait that does not require immediate positive feedback. Grit is such a necessary component in a progressive Black man's life. You have to be hard, resilient, and sometimes out right gritty in order to persevere through life's obstacles and achieve your goals and objectives. An interesting study of positive psychology by doctoral candidate Angela Duckworth determined *grit* to be the premier determinant amongst indicators of long term success. Oh how Black men need to reflect the attributes of Grit. Grit in combination with a clear objective and goal will absolutely aid as a fuel for our passionate agenda and catapult the progression of Black community in America.

"In the beginning God created the heavens and the earth.... Then God said, "Let us make man in our image, according to our likeness..." – Genesis Verse 1

G is also for Godly - The creator and ruler of the universe and the source of all moral authority; the supreme. There is no need to go in full detail of the necessity of God and godliness as perspective principles for growth, because it is ridiculously obvious. Thomas Kelly wrote, "Our deepest need is not food and clothing and shelter, important as they are. It is God!" Without God as a setting for godly principles and priorities, there is no reason to have any principles or priorities. There is no life without God and any priority of life set without God will be of null usage based upon its disorderly arrangement and disorganization. God as a principle is simply an organizational guide applicable to all of life. God is the core of all principles. God is the principle of all principles. God is the principle! God is definitely good!

"Prayer is not asking. It is a longing of the soul. It is daily admission of one's weakness. It is better in prayer to have a heart without words than words without a heart." -Mahatma Gandhi

---

H is for heart. The heart is a vital pump-like organ of the muscular anatomy that oxygenates and circulates blood throughout the body. When a heart fails to pump and circulate blood— the body will die.

The heart is also considered the center of person's total personality. It is especially the center of a person's total personality in reference to his intuitions, feelings, connections, and emotions.

To me these four functions of personality are relative to the functions of the heart's four chambers. One chamber is meant to process and purify, two to distribute, and one as a return to the heart's circulatory system.

Anyone that has ever watched the 2001 movie The Lion King is familiar with its theme "the circle of life." The heart and its distributive attributes represent the driving force in our world's true circle of life. All of life is based upon circles, circulatory systems, and spherical principles. What you put in is what you get out. What you reap is what you have sewn. And what goes around comes around. I think that each of these may reference to the state of a man's heart. If a man is of good heart, his motives and intentions are pure, and the displays of his heart throughout his lifetime will undoubtedly return back to him in the same condition. But in relative contrast, if a man's heart is ill, his motives and intentions are tainted and unhealthy, and the displays of his heart throughout his lifetime will undoubtedly return back to him in the same condition. It's the circulatory system of life — or as The Lion King has taught us -"the circle of life."

A good heart in good health spreads healthy blood throughout the body the same way a man of good heart spreads good will throughout his community. And a good community promotes men of good heart the same way that good diet and exercise promote healthy blood, blood vessels, and the overall heart's health.

Everything in life starts and returns with the heart. We undoubtedly reap in a spherical accordance to our hearts condition. This is why it is important to consciously assess and monitor its condition on a regular basis. It is even more important to consciously assess and monitor the things that may be affecting that condition. I believe that the prevalence of distrust and jealously amongst Black men are the telling symptoms of ill heart conditions. Traits such as jealously and distrust are like salt and sodium for the heart. Both are unnecessary and unhealthy consumptions that may cause complications and deteriorate an other-wise healthy system.

I think that along with high salt and sodium consumption — jealousy, distrust, and malicious discrediting directly correlate to Black men's high susceptibility to cardiovascular diseases and cancerous deaths.

The Centers for Disease Control and Preventions report heart diseases and cancers as the number one and number two killers of Black men in every year since 1970. I believe this, as well as homicide rates, and the prevalence of hypertension and diabetes, to be blatant evidence that Black men practice habitually destructive behaviors stemming from (and returning to) their own heart's condition.

I believe you are what is on your heart and there is no exception to the principle. Every man and every woman will directly reap exactly what they have nurtured on their own heart. This is why it is so essential to exercise loving gestures and to take in healthy consumptions of positive literature for you hearts consideration on a daily basis. Healthy habits promote a healthy heart condition spiritually, the same as healthy habits promote a healthy heart condition physically. It's the same principle. It's the same heart. It's the same circulatory system. And it's the same circulation of life.

I think the principle of heart is so essential to the progressive growth of Black men, Black families, Black communities, and the ideal of a Black Nationalism. Because what life can any man live without a healthy heart to sustain him? What life can any family live without the heart to maintain it? What life can any community comprise without the heart to drive it? And lastly, what nation has ever arisen without the heart to try it?

It takes a lot of heart to use your heart. This is why many people may be so reluctant to give it freely to others. A weak heart may hide itself in-order not to hurt. A strong heart has been exercised, beaten up, used, abused, hurt, broken, stabbed, ached, exhausted, disappointed, and denied. A weak heart shells itself and avoids exposure to these issues. But a strong heart always has the courage (heart) to expose itself and its vulnerability for love. A strong heart, despite wears and tears, always has the courage (heart) to try itself and love again. The heart is bold, assertive, vigorous, relentless, persistent, resilient, and courageous. The strongest man in the world is simply a mimicking reflection of his own heart's qualities. It takes a lot of strong heart to follow after your own heart. In my heart, I feel that no heart should hide itself from the love it was meant to give, receive, and achieve. It is unnatural and weak — and a weak heart is no heart at all. Every mature person knows that love may hurt. But only the strong (hearts) survive. To give and receive love and nurture is the purpose of the heart. A weak heart that has avoided love in order not to hurt has failed its purpose. And when a heart fails the body dies (heart disease).

Don't be afraid to use your heart. Don't be afraid to give your heart. In the case with God your heart may be all you have to give. Don't be afraid to give him all of it. Don't be afraid to lead with your heart. Don't be afraid to follow your heart. Don't be afraid to strengthen your heart by giving love that may not be immediately reciprocated. The universe is lovingly designed after a heart's circulatory system. Any love you may produce and give (pulmonary) will undoubtedly return (vena cava). Don't be afraid to give your love and don't be afraid to receive love. You have to learn to trust with your heart, in your heart, with all of your heart.

The condition of your heart should be one of the most vital concerns in a man's life. As much as physical exercise, vegetables, literature, love, water, wine, and smooth music should be a daily intake for his own heart's health — each Black man should make a conscious effort to exercise and display the attributes of a good healthy heart toward those in his community who may need his vital love and support for *their* own heart's health. The strength of heart is such a wonderful gift for a man to give because it will always be loyally return to him, his community, and his children's community in the exact condition that he gave it. Your heart is good. Don't be afraid to use it.

The ABC's of a Black Man's Principles

"If you do not tell the truth about yourself you
cannot tell it about other people." - Virginia Woolf

H is for Honesty and Humility – Honesty is the quality of being truthful and sincere. Humility is a modesty or meekness with a lowly view of one's own importance. Honesty and humility are two principles that will always go unappreciated, unnoticed, and unheralded. There is no reward for humility. There is no prize for honesty. There is only the confident integrity of oneself. Principles are not trophies or show pieces. Neither attribute will make you a famous man. They are not useful to gain any attention. Honesty and humility are simply the nuts, bolts, screws, and nails in the building of a strong man. No one ever pays any attention to the small screws and staples in a beautifully crafted home. It is the accumulation of small uncompromised principles that make the whole man respectably admirable. Honesty and humility build integrity and integrity builds confidence, strength and consistency. These characteristics in turn, make up a well rounded man of strong unwavering qualities.

"The best way to not feel hopeless is to get up and do something. Don't wait for good things to happen to you. If you go out and make some good things happen, you will fill the world with hope, you will fill yourself with hope." - Barack Obama

I is for Initiative - Initiative is the ability to assess and initiate things independently. Initiative is also the power or opportunity to act or take charge before others do.

Many people identify themselves by different qualities. Speaking for myself, my initiative is my identifying quality. I feel that I am my initiative. I am my initiative even to my fault. When you initiate, things become the doings of who you are, and what you have done as an accountable person—faults included.

I could never imagine living my life without any initiative as some people do. I've even grown slightly disdain and dismissive of people with solely responsive traits.

People with initiative are more audacious, accountable, and responsible. Overall they are more progressive, and in my opinion— more fun. Initiators don't mind making mistakes and don't judge others of that same initiative because, they understand what initiative entails.

Responsive personalities love and hate initiators. They love initiators because they can hide all of their faults behind him or her. They can always say he or she did it. It's always an initiators fault, and most times initiators will absolutely accept it. Who wouldn't want such a perfect scapegoat for inequity?

Responsive personalities never really win, and never really lose, because they never really shoot. They just usually take what's given to them, or what they've earned, and tend to blame, point, complain, justify, and excuse. Innocence is good to uphold but it's just not at all who I am — I'd rather be accountable.

I love to be proactive in the pursuit of my personal growth. I love to take the blame, be pointed at, and offer no explanatory excuse or justification. I love to take accountability for my fault. It's so empowering and surprisingly educational in its consequence.

My Initiative has taught me so many things and created so many opportunities throughout my life. Some from absolutely nothing! When you simply respond, you have to wait for opportunities to be presented.

The ABC's of a Black Man's Principles

Even then responsive people don't tend to recognize its presence or its presentation. Unless something is totally given to you, you'd still have to initiate some form of acceptance.

The thing about being solely responsive is that most times even when opportunities are presented and hopefully recognized–a lack of initiative will limit or even minimize the size of the opportunity to the proportion of its presentation.

As an exact contrast initiative not only makes opportunities... it may maximize the potential of that opportunity.

I love to be around people of this type of trait. There is always some engagement in proactive activity and you never know when something significant may manifest.

In the case for Black men, I would not only like to see them initiate successful lives as individuals, but I would like for Black men to initiate a provocative agenda towards their optimal success entirely. I damn sure wouldn't mind being the initiator of such an initiative.

"The integrity of the upright will guide them..."
- Proverbs 11: 3

I is for Integrity – Integrity is the quality of being honest and having strong moral principles and moral uprightness. The integrity of a man should not be compromised! This is what integrity is in fact. There is no point in building yourself as a strong man of strong principles if you are to compromise those principles under pressure, when it is convenient, or even opportunistic. Of all the principles, this may be the hardest, because it is such a constant internal maintenance. Many men have built themselves and then killed themselves as significant social figures based upon their integrity. It, as trust, is very slowly earned and only lost once.

Chapter Four

JKL's

The ABC's of a Black Man's Principles

"When I do good, I feel Good. When I do bad, I feel bad. That's my religion." – Abraham Lincoln

---

J **is for Just** - Just is defined as having a basis in or conforming to fact or reason. This is a really basic principle. Every decision or action should be based upon some type of just cause or consideration. Men, who base themselves upon a consistent reasoning, stand much higher, and much stronger, than men who react based upon their sporadic inclinations and circumstantial emotion. Don't just be a man, be a just man!

"Knowledge isn't power — workable knowledge is power!"- Melvin Ruffin

K is for Knowledge - The term knowledge is to have understanding through experience and other relative intelligence. I believe you are what you know. Even if you are uneducated, it is essentially wise to be knowledgeable of that which you do not know. The most important knowledge is knowledge of God. Secondarily is the knowledge of self.

Knowledge of self is the conscious awareness of who you are, what you are like, and how you relate to the world. A keen knowledge of one's self enables a person to assess himself and his environment accurately, to make the according decisions necessary for his survival and his flourishing.

An example of a directive map at the mall comes to mind. The "YOU ARE HERE" is the most important thing to understand. From that point you can figure what you are close to, where you are going, and about how far you are from your objective destination. The same is true of Black men as individuals and as a collective group. You have to know yourself before you can grow yourself. Knowledge is a principle key to that growth.

"..And Though I have all faith, so that I could
remove mountains, but have not love, I am nothing."
- 1 Corinthians 13:2

L is for Loving– The expression *loving* is defined to show, feel, and indicate love and affection. It is an adjective form of the verb love, which means to cherish, caress, desire, and have affection for. This is almost a cliché of principles. There is nothing in the world without love. Everything needs nurturing. This is especially for the things with intentions of growing. The growth of a Black community, or any community for that matter, cannot and should not be done without the principle characteristics of love and loving people.

A Black man not only needs to be a loving man, he also needs a loving man to encouragingly nurture the loving growth within himself. How can anyone grow love if they do not know love? This is one of the profound principles that I feel are urgently essential to the mending and empowerment of Black men.

As one of my mentors reviewed some principle points in my book he repeatedly stated, "Yea, Black men are definitely lacking that!" I sharply disagreed that we are lacking anything, and that we just need to encourage and nurture growth. But, if a Black man is lacking any of this books principles this, may be the sole one.

Sixty-five percent of Black males have grown up in households where there father did not live. I'm not saying that's a problem. I'm saying that's the problem. If a child never learns to love himself from a man he cannot learn to love others as a man. If a man cannot love others as a man he cannot maintain, grow, and direct a household.

Today's woman is way too independent to need a man that doesn't know how to love her and her child. But! Oh how today's woman needs and wants a loving man for her and *their* child. Love is not dismissive. A loving black man would not resolve to separate so quickly and commonly from his unit.

It does not matter how strong a man is. The strength in him is the love in him. If no man has ever instilled, nurtured, and sharpened the love in him, those responsible for that responsibility have emasculated him. He is powerless to withstand the world's satanic attack of Black family. If a man knows no love in him, he won't even fight to maintain that family. That is why 65 percent of black homes are broken — because there is no sustaining love to even provoke a fight of Black men (the strongest men on earth) to maintain it. That is very sad. I'm not saying that's *a* problem. I am saying that's *the* problem!

Love suffers all things, love endures all things. Surely it would endure the turbulence every young family must go through. Love does not boast. Love bears all things, believes all things, and most of all love never fails.

A Black man could have all the principle in this book, all the wisdom, and all the faith to move mountains but if he has not love, he has nothing (NO THINGS).

"Leadership is not about titles, positions or
flowcharts. It is about one life influencing another."
- John C. Maxwell

L is also for Leadership – Leadership is the act of leading, the ability to lead, and the function or position of a leader. Leadership is a process of social influence or the organization of a group to achieve a goal. If you were to ask ten people to define leadership, you will likely hear ten different answers. For this reason, leadership can be a wide array of things, with many different types and levels. Leadership can be a talent, or a developed exercise. The main idea of leadership is the ability to obtain followers. So leadership in all its illusiveness is simply one's ability to influence. Leadership is basically one's ability to influence his followers.

Everybody at one time or another is influenced by, and influential to, someone. Parents influence children, teachers influence students, and managers influence employees. In these examples; parents, teachers, and managers, become leaders. Each leader has a responsibility to his follower. A leader's leadership capabilities depend highly upon his acknowledgement and acceptance of responsibility to his followers. Good leadership acknowledges a responsibility (accountability) and then takes the actions necessary to fulfill that responsibility (initiative).

The ABC's of a Black Man's Principles

Leadership qualities are what actually make a leader influential. Integrity, magnanimity, humility, dedication, transparency, creativity, assertiveness, and humor are all traits of leadership that determine the ability of a leader.

The present of Black men should acknowledge, as a responsibility, their obligations as the influential leadership to the future of young Black men who will so desperately need them. Whether in business, church, school or just life we all are chosen to be leaders at one time or another. Black men must all grow our skills as leaders and accept the responsibility of leadership roles in order to be successful in our community and future generation.

"The strength of a family, like the strength of an army, is in its loyalty to each other." -Mario Puzo

L is lastly for Loyal - Loyal is an adjective primarily defined as an allegiance to one's homeland, government, or sovereign. It is secondarily defined as a faithfulness to a person, ideal, custom, cause, or duty. To be loyal and to have loyalty are extremely deep principles. Only in the depths of a man can you find his true loyalties.

The loyalties of a man derive from his core. More specifically, the loyalties of a man derive from his heart. A loyal man is a man that has devoted himself to something or someone with his whole heart.

As a comparative question — how important is the heart to the living body? It's pretty important huh? I believe that loyalty in a man's life is equally vital as having a beating heart. A man with no heart has no loyalty, and a man with no loyalty has no heart. A man with no heart is a dead man, and I believe a man of no loyalty should be too. That may seem harsh in conveyance, but I believe that the principle of loyalty in a loyal man is as vital as life and death. A loyal man's loyalty can only be to things that he may, and, or will die for. A man's loyalty is a pledge of allegiance with his life, for the duration of his life. This is why disloyalty should be considered such a despicable trait amongst men. The declaration of loyalty to a person, ideal, custom, cause or duty (and especially to God) — should be a whole-hearted allegiance of your life, for the entire duration of your life— to the death.

"Until death do you part, "those things you give your heart and loyalties to (friends, family, ideals, customs, duties, lovers, country, God)—should forever have it. And you should forever be true to that loyalty. Consider it like a marriage to your loyalties. Not like so many failed marriages of today, but as a marriage was intended—forever.

Women may equate their loyalty (singular) with more of a physical exclusiveness, or a sexual monogamy, but the loyalties (plural) of a man are in his spirit, and in the allegiance of his heart. In a loyal relationship, a loyal woman aligns her heart/loyalties with those same loyalties of her man and vice versa (unison). This is why it is vitally imperative that a man and woman both align his and her heart/loyalties with God's will. The alignment of God's will on earth is initiated in the loyal hearts of loyal men and then trickles down to their loyal women and their loyal children too.

I think each Black man should be loyally dedicated to aligning himself within the will of God. Prioritizing loyalty to God enables the

55

proper configuration in our subsidiary loyalties to each-other, our relationships, our objectives, our communities and in our responsibilities. Loyalty is good. Be loyal to God.

Chapter Five

MNO's

"Excessive sorrow laughs. Excessive joy weeps."
                        - William Blake

M **is for Moderate** - Merriam- Webster defines *moderate* as avoiding extremes of behavior or expression or observing reasonable limits. Kept or keeping within reasonable or proper limits. Alongside of accountability and balance--moderation is one of my favorite principles. I think this is one of the greatest principles a man can learn and carry through his life.

The principle of moderate is so practical and so applicable to every instance, approach, or situation. Everything should be done in moderation. We all know by now that everything is bad for you. Every time you turn on the news they have new research to tell you that the food you've been eating your whole life is basically going to kill you. But in a rational truth— too much of anything can really kill you! In a more precise quote by Cassandra Clare, she says, "Too much of anything can destroy you." This is applicable in habitual behavior, diet, sex, work, recreation and even consumption. Andrew Thornton was a 44 year old active man who actually died of excessive water consumption! Seventeen pints in eight hours to be exact. But this is just an extreme case to reinforce that everything should be done in moderation. Moderation is good.

> "Negligence is the rust of the soul that corrodes through all her best resolves." - Owen Feltham

N is for Negligence. A person has acted negligently if he or she has departed from the conduct expected of a reasonably prudent person acting under similar circumstances. In a court of law negligence entails very serious consequence and is even considered a justifiable tort (a wrongful act that results in injury to another person's, property, reputation, and the like. The injured party is then entitled to compensation.) Negligence is conduct that falls below the standards of behavior established by law for the protection of others against unreasonable risk of harm.

Negligence is obviously not a principle or characteristic you would like to obtain, develop, or be guilty of. It is however, something that Black men should be, or become, aware to. Negligence' root word *neglect* means to pay no attention, or too little attention to. To neglect is to disregard, slight, or omit through indifference or carelessness.

I think that Black men are guilty to a high degree of negligence. They have neglected the responsibility to make any compensative provision for the next generation of Black youth. Everyone knows the epidemic proportion of absentee fathers in the home. But where is the effort to resolve, amend, balance, or even compensate for this disparity?

Negligence is a terrible trait to be ignorant to. It also has very serious consequential effects upon the community. The negligence of a father can do great harm to a child that may not be evident until expressed later through aggressive behavior. The same is to be said for the Black community. The negligence of a community can do great harm to its blossoming youth. These harmful side, and after effects may not be evident until expressed later through their aggressive, unproductive, or even their own negligent behavior.

The grand effects of negligence cannot be accurately documented nor surveyed because no negligent person is ever going to take accountability for their negligence. They are especially not going to say that they are at fault for the repercussions of their negligence. That is why it is important to grow and raise awareness to the terrible effects of negligent behavior and conduct. This principle is an essential principle for this generation of Black men and the next to learn, correct, and avoid. The responsibility of Black men, to take accountability for Black men, has to at some point be officially owned and initiated. That time is now.

*"When being objective, we can transcend and look
back at our constructs with powerful clarity…"*
-Jay Woodman

O is for Objective – Objective is defined as something that one's efforts or actions are intended to attain or accomplish. Your objective is your purpose. You have to have an objective in life. If there is no purpose for your life there is no direction for your life. Where are you going if you have no direction? It's like getting up every day and getting ready, making coffee, taking a shower, getting in your car, and driving around your city making random rights and lefts — where will you end up? Who knows? But surely not any where you want or intended. You have to have an objective to anything you do. What is the outcome you are looking for? What is the goal? If Black men can apply this principle to everyday life, everyday task, and then to everything we do within that day — I believe we truly can progress objectively for ourselves. An objective is mandatory.

Chapter Six

P&Q's

"He that can have patience can have what he will."
– Benjamin Franklin

P is for patience – Patience is the capacity to accept or tolerate delay, trouble, or suffering without getting angry or upset. Patience is the state of endurance under difficult circumstances.

As Attention Deficit / Hyperactivity Disorder or (ADHD) is quickly becoming the most common neurobehavioral disorder in America; patience in today's world is a fragile notion. But even in its scarcity; patience still has always been, and will always be — a positive virtue in life.

Every valuable possession or accomplishment in life may take time and dedication. Impatient people give up on relationships, goals, values, education, and many other things that require patience. But patient people find ways to proactively wait and give things the proper time to materialize. This type of patience enables them to enjoy more of the benefits that an impatient person may have forfeited in their haste.

Patience is also relative to the substance of perseverance. Our current society thrives on the desire to be gratified instantly. Nobody has the time or the patience to simply wait. Many people have developed a

63

low tolerance for any type of delay and as a result, the perseverance required for substantial progress is almost extinct.

Anything worth having, any relationship worth building, and any business endeavor worth pursuing — will all require patience and perseverance. The old cliché — "Rome wasn't built in one day," is true. It may have actually taken around 318,000 days for Rome to reach its peak.

The intended point is that nothing great is established over night and neither will any significant social progress for Black men. The unification of Black men for a collective Black agenda in America will take time and perseverance.

We have to develop the patience to stay the proactive course and persevere towards the benefits of quality character and integrative principles.

Everything takes time and everybody hates lines — but in life there are no shortcuts — and sometimes you will just have to wait. Patience is good!

> "Life is 10% what happens to me and 90% how I react to it." – John C. Maxwell

P **is for Perspective** – A perspective is defined as the subjective evaluation of relative significance. That might be a lot to swallow — so, it is more simply defined as a point of view. It is also the mental ability to perceive things in their actual interrelations or comparative importance. That also might be a lot to chew — so, it is simply your minds digestion of an experience or occurrence. I really want my reader to take the point that perspective is a mental relation of interpretation; and that everything in life is relative or subjective to each one's own perspective.

Perspective is everything and everything is perspective — especially in your own life. Each person is in a different place at different points in life. The way you deal with things is dependent upon how you have seen things. Nothing else is more influential in reactive or proactive behavior than a person's perspective. This is why I feel perspective, and the maturation of it, to be so important.

It is very important to read, converse, relate and meditate upon other's perspective in order to fully broaden and develop one's own.

An example could be a single dimension media versus mutli-dimension media. Imagine a camera set at a directly frontal angle. This cameras view is limited to a frontal view therefore, can only reflect frontal images and only have a frontal perspective. Now this same frontal camera's view in conjunction with an elevated rear camera would combine for a much better reflection of the actual image. Does that make sense in relation to perspective? Now imagine a third camera from a third angle and so on. The point is, when you consider the vantages of other people's perspective in combination with your own, it makes for a wider, deeper, multi-dimensioned interpretation that is much more precise and definite. It is parallel to the picture difference in Star Wars on VHS and Transformers on hi-def blue ray.

So in my perspective as a Black man, I love to consider the perspective of other Black men as well as Black women, White women, White men, Latinos, Latinas, Asian's and as many different people (youth are people too) that I feel may have a relevant and relative perspective to my own.

I believe that Black communities should be self sufficient and independent as a selective option aside, but definitely not in any seclusion or exclusion, from other races. It is very well my perspective to borrow others perspective in formation of my own. I absolutely believe we can learn from each other. I think it is imperative that Black men open themselves to learn from other races in order to more clearly define themselves. Even this book of principles was derived from many relative principles that I learned from families of White and Latino men.

In the end the core of all our differences derives from perspective. I feel that Black men's perspective is the hardest to relate to because it has for so long been singular dimensioned and blurry. My perspective is that we work to develop a better focus and multi dimensioned collective image by borrowing, sharing, and considering the perspectives of our White, Latino, and Asian brothers. If perspective is everything, why not consider everybody's? Wider is better!

"Be practical as well as generous in your ideals.
Keep your eyes on the stars, but remember to keep
your feet on the ground." – Theodore Roosevelt

P is also for **Practicality** – Practicality is derived from the root word practice. To practice procedures designed and adapted for applicable uses and actual usage is to be practical. Practicality may be my absolutely favorite principle. In lack of others, I've applied this principle to so many situations, dilemmas, and difficult decisions. I think of all the principles in this book, practicality, is absolutely the most practical. I simply try to maintain, prioritize, or devote an exclusive focus to the things that are useful to me and my objective.

Just do what makes the most sense and is in the most accordance with your objective. Prioritize your objectives and make decisions that are subordinate to the actualization of your goals. Being practical is so easy and so clear and the efficient benefit is usually so immediate that it is my favorite principle to practice.

"Without a struggle there can be no progress."
– Frederick Douglass

P is lastly for **Progressive** – Progressive is the adjectival form of progress. The word progress is defined as a movement toward a goal, a further stage, or a higher level. To be progressive is to advocate for change, improvement, reform, and development all in the objective movement toward a goal. The importance of progression in a man is rudiment. A progressive man is constantly looking for ways to improve and welcoming the changes necessary for improvement. A progressive man is constantly bettering himself.

The world may ask a lot of a man in his lifetime. I would ask nothing more of a man than to be progressive in his mind, his spirit, his worth, and in his self! We are all imperfect, born into different imperfect situations. All a man can do in his life is to strive for better and look to improve upon his self continually.

"Quality begins on the inside.... Then works its way out" – Bob Moawad

Q is for Quality – Quality is an inherent or distinguishing characteristic or a superiority of kind. My favorite definition of quality is: character with respect to grade of excellence or fineness. You can tell everything about a person from their qualities and values (Especially if they have none).

People whom strive for quality always give their best, try their best, expect their best, and want their best. Everything you do should be in your best effort. You should never settle for "good enough." Why wouldn't you be the best kind of person you could possibly be? I'd really like to encourage my readers to aspire to be of an exceptional, internal make-up, and distinguish themselves with principles and superior characteristics. Don't just be men, be quality men. Don't just be a man, be a man of quality.

"You are what you are responsible for."
– Mark Anthony Howard

R **is for Responsibility** – Responsibility is the quality or state of being morally, legally, or mentally accountable. I feel that the principle of responsibility is *umbrella'd* under the principle of accountability. But I would just hate to omit such a weighty word as responsibility from a book of principles.

I truly believe that you are what you are responsible for. Each man's responsibilities and his handle of those responsibilities are a complete reflection of the man he is. The measure of every man is based upon the scale of his responsibility. The greater the man, the greater his responsibilities and vice-versa. It is a direct correlation with no short cuts. Every man should take full accountability for himself, his family, and the direction of that family, and then extend himself outward into the community. Black men should be taking greater responsibility for their past, present, and the progression into the future. Responsibility is good.

"If money is your hope for independence you will
never have it. The only real security that a man will
have in this world is a reserve of knowledge,
experience, and ability." - Henry Ford

R is for Reserve – Reserve means to keep back as for further use or a special purpose. It is to keep for one self or retain. A reserve is keeping of one's feelings, thoughts or affairs to oneself. A man's reserve is also his strength. My father always taught me to "Keep an ace" up my sleeve. I found this very wise and practical. It is neither wise nor practical, to always reveal and communicate your every thought or agenda that you may have. A cliché is to say that "actions speak louder than words," but I like to think that doing is more important than saying. And sometimes, it is just frankly much more advantageous to think, absorb, and reserve one's thoughts than it may be to speak, respond, and reveal them all.

A reserve is practical in minimizing the futility and triviality of arguments and confrontation while maintaining an objective focus on the important priorities.

When I think of reserve and its greatest example, I think of the man Jackie Robinson. Jackie Robinson displayed the greatest amount of not only restraint, but reserve during the integration project of the late

1940's and 50's. What people misconstrue of Jackie Robinson is that he was mild tempered and quiet. The exact opposite was the case.

The strongly opinionated Jackie Robinson exercised the greatest amount of reserve in his lack of response to prejudice, disrespect, and hatred. The bigger picture of completing his grand agenda was much more important to Jackie than responding to each trivial insult, threat, and slight thrown toward him to derail it. A principle of reserve is also necessary for the completion of your own grand agendas as well. A reserve is good!

"In a poetical sense, you have to open a book to open your mind and open your mind to open a book as well." - Mark Anthony Howard (The Gritz)

R **is also for Receptive** - The adjective receptive is defined to be mentally open to, able to, or capable of receiving something; especially signals, stimuli, or instruction. A definition of receptive I find most relevant is the willingness to consider or accept new suggestions or ideas.

As a principle, you have to be receptive to have any type of success in life (Especially to God). You have to be able to receive new ideas and new instructions. You definitely have to be open to receiving them. The consideration of new ideas and alternative perspectives is the entire foundation of personal growth. The most important thing a person can do to enhance themselves, and to become more receptive, is read (Especially God's word in The Bible)!

Reading is one of the most essential pastimes ever created. It is essentially so, because it is not just a pastime, it is a life necessity. Donalyn Miller wrote in her book "The Book Whisperer:"

"Reading changes your life. Reading unlocks worlds unknown or forgotten, taking travelers around the world and through time. Reading

helps you escape the confines of school and

pursue your own education. Through

characters – real and fictitious – reading shows

you how to be a better human being."

Reading is such a necessity of life because it plants seeds through your senses, fertilizes your heart, waters your soul, shines sunlight on your mind, and grows you. It shows you how, when, and where to grow, and growth should be our entire purpose. Growth, above all, is what makes you a better person.

The reading of a just one good book can be completely pivotal in a life of any reader. Malcolm X contributed his entire reformation from criminal to intellect to books and said, "What people don't realize is that how a man's whole life can be change by one book." That is entire point of a book; the complete consideration of a life changing ideal! Its entire premise is built around the consideration of new ideas and the writers hope, that its reader will consider those new ideas. Of course though, you have to first be receptive to books before the ideas they contain may reform you. You have to be receptive to new ideas in order to receive the applicable instructions that a book may propose. In a poetical sense, you have to open a book to open your mind, and open your mind to open a book as well.

Lastly, to complete my point of receptiveness, I would even go as far as saying to open your ears, spirit, and heart most importantly. To be receptive is usually in reference to the mind. But I believe it is much more dependent upon the condition of the heart and spirit. A receptive heart opens the mind much further than it would be capable of doing on its own. And a receptive spirit allows a person to fully receive God's and the entire universe's intentions for your personal direction and growth. All of these entail the principle of receptive; the mind, ears, heart, and spirit. You have to want to receive — and be looking to receive — growth, in all its forms, in order to be optimally receptive to it.

The ABC's of a Black Man's Principles

"America needs to relearn a lost discipline, self confident relentlessness..." – Lance Morrow

R is lastly for **Relentless** – To Relent is to give in, concede, or to quit. To be relentless is the opposite of such. To be relentless is to be steady, persistent, and conceding to nothing. A man of a relentless principle will stop at nothing short of his objectives. Nothing or no one can stop him from progressing toward his goals. Any obstacle, opposition, or adversity is simply turbulence in his flight through his life.

Relentlessness is a great principle to have. It also is a very personal principle of my own. I almost want to write this as a dedication to myself. Sometimes life is a tough and overbearing thing to endure through (especially for the struggling young Black male). There are many difficult situations with many different pressures, obstacles, tragedies, distractions and disappointments. These things are a depressing weight upon any man's heart. What I found in my own life is that for each negative occurrence and let down, there has to be a countering pick up — or pull — back towards positivity. The more negativity there is in your life — the more focused and dedicated you have to be to positively compensate.

77

The ABC's of a Black Man's Principles

In order to be successful you will have to persevere through failure. Failure is always an option. Failure always offers itself as the first and most convenient option available when a person is experiencing difficulties. It always offers itself as opposition to your success as a man. In order to succeed you have be relentless in the pursuance of your goals and objectives. If you are going to positively progress in life, you have to be relentlessly ambitious, motivated, and progressive.

My favorite quote from the great motivational speaker Eric Thomas says, "When you want success as bad as you want to breathe, then you will succeed!" I encourage my young Black readers to breathe relentlessly, strive relentlessly, and thrive relentlessly.

Chapter Seven

STU's

The ABC's of a Black Man's Principles

S is for Self-Sufficiency- Self-sufficiency is a hard principle to follow. Life is hard and sometimes, it is much easier to look toward others for dependency. This is where the principle of self-sufficiency is purposeful. A man has to learn to stand and maintain for himself, and by himself, before he should start a family that may be so dependent upon him and his ability to provide for its sufficiency. How can a family lean upon a man that is incapable of standing upon his own? It is far too often and almost the norm that young Black men jump from baby to baby's father. Each young man should have the proper time to develop in each stage. From an embryo to an infant, to a toddler, to a child, to an adolescent, to a teenager. Each stage is essential for the next; from a teenager to an adult from an adult, finally, to an independent adult. Just as an embryonic stage is crucial to a person's development this independent or self sufficient stage is also a very important developmental stage of life. Each man's life should have self-sufficiency as a prioritized stage.

Once a man has developed himself as self sufficient then he may look to move into marriage and then into parenthood. In order to be a successful person one has to be orderly. Black families are failing simply in relation to disorder. My grandfather, Ernest Howard Sr. used to tell me about "The cart before the horse." I hated how every conversation I would have about my goals and what I wanted to do with my life would provoke the same response, "you can't put the cart before the horse boy." That cliché still aggravates me to this day, but it is so true!

Everything has its order and its organizational procedure. You cannot expect to be successful as a man, a woman, a person, a group, a team, a unit, or a people if you continually mis-order your life's conduct, stages, and organizational procedures. Mis-order is disorder and disorder is chaos. A chaotic life-style is a sure way to remain unsuccessful and unproductive.

A man's self-sufficiency is his independence. Black people cannot, and will not, ever grow to self-sufficiency and independence if its men are incapable of such principles individually.

"I think it is important to see spiritual as a part of
physical, rather than to separate these two
dimensions of our reality. It is all one. Spirit
represents that which we cannot validate with our
senses." – Wayne W. Dyer

S **is for Spirit** – The elements of spirit and spirituality are vast and complex but your spirit is most simply your soul. The word spirit comes from the Latin word spiritus which means breath. It is defined as the nonphysical part of a person that may seat emotions and the definitive qualities that form a person's character. The spirit is also defined as the central part of a person's life, will, thinking, and feeling.

The definition I find most relevant to my own spirit is Merriam-Webster's definition. Spirit is a vital principle held to give life to physical organisms; a supernatural being or essence.

The spirit is obviously very difficult to define. I also find it very difficult to explain and convey literally. Here is my try...

The world is much more than its concrete appearance. Some things have to be sensed within, and sometimes passed, logic. So much of the world is experienced through physical senses. When we interact with other people we relate primarily through our five physical senses: sight, touch, hear, smell, and sometimes taste. But I truly believe that it is much more important to relate and perceive spiritually. I think our spirituality may be our sixth sense.

But the spirit as a sixth sense is false in significant order. The spirit should be prioritized as our first sense. The spirit should be prioritized as our first sense in all of our relation to the world.

Think of this as a leading example. If you want to speak to a man in a Latin country, you may have to communicate verbally in some form of Latin. If you wanted to communicate to a woman in an African country, you may have to communicate some form of African dialect. If you wanted to communicate with a woman in Japan, you may have to speak Japanese. If you want to speak to a man in Vietnam, you would have to speak Vietnamese. If you want to speak to man of the universe, what language or dialect would you have to speak?

The answer is a universal language and it is not a language communicated verbally. God is a universal being that communicates through spirit. You will never have a verbal conversation with God because mere words are not important to God. What it is important to God is spirit. God is the almighty nurture of everything spiritual. Those things that wish to be considered within his universal care must learn to communicate spiritually. The same as children must learn to communicate the dialect of their providing parent, each universal child must learn to communicate spiritually to in-order the provisions of our father God.

I think if Black men learn to consciously prioritize and communicate themselves through positive spirit, then they will free themselves of the physical weights which may have bound them socially as a progressive group. You cannot bind a spirit if the spirit wills not to be bound. The spirit of a Black man has been proven to proceed and succeed bondage. I pray with my spirit, that the spirit of Black men is able to succeed vanity and selfishness as well.

I think as Black men learn to consciously prioritize and communicate amongst themselves through positive spirit, then they will free themselves of some self binding attributes that may have also restricted them from a progressive growth as a group socially. A conscious prioritization of spiritual communication will not only free Black men of social binding, it would free Black men from restrictive bondage mentally, financially, emotionally, physically, and most importantly to God... spiritually as well. Your spirit is good. Communicate it

.

"If there is no struggle, there is no progress. Those who profess to favor freedom, and yet depreciate agitation, are men who want crops without plowing up the ground...

...This struggle may be a moral one; or it may be a physical one; or it may be both moral and physical' but must be a struggle." -Fredrick Douglass

S is for Struggle – A struggle is a strenuous effort in the face of difficulties or opposition. To struggle is to make a forceful or violent effort to get free of restraint, or from constriction. This principle is one that even I may struggle to convey literally. I especially struggle to convey any positive encouragement or motivation toward enduring a struggle.

Struggling simply sucks! It is no fun and there aint shit glamorous or attractive about it.

At many times, I feel my own personal struggles have completely consumed my morale and life. I have struggled with so many different things, at so many different times (sometimes at the same time) that I feel my life is best described as a struggle. I've mostly struggled with myself and the issues that concern me. But I have also struggled with my perception of women, faith, God, love, school, religion, authority, friendship, family, efficacy, consistency, focus, sexual appetite, mental health, homelessness, self-worth, self-esteem, self-employment, abuse, neglect, respect, violence, wild impulses, comprehension, principle, suicide, and a bunch of other shit too.

The truth I have found is that every man will at some point in his life be met with a struggle. What distinguishes a man is his response to, and perseverance through— that struggle.

A man that embraces his struggle will be much more considerate of things that may positively or negatively affect it, and therefore increase his chances of persevering through his struggle.

But the harsh reality of struggle is that even a man that embraces his struggle may not always earn the benefit of overcoming it. There is no guarantee that any man will succeed in a struggle. Sometimes struggles overwhelm us and we lose.

Many people die every day in a losing struggle against life's many ills. Things such cancers, diseases, bullying, debt, depression, domestic violence, drug addiction, the contemplation of suicide, and many other stressors may be life-threatening internal struggles that people are battling against daily.

Each person is different— but struggle is an evil in life that everybody faces.

It's very sad how insensitive, and unconcerned, many people may be in consideration to the struggles that others may be enduring. In a society were financial success is everyone's passionate goal; it seems no-one has time to compassionately aid in the struggle of another.

In my own life I feel that I have discouraged many friendships with the melancholy conveyance of my struggles.

Perhaps one of the most dis-heartening of all the dis-heartening ills of enduring a struggle is the isolation it encourages. It's like an added struggle to your struggle and it hurts your heart (the one thing you need most to fight) directly.

But for all the negativity that a struggle involves, I feel it is as necessary in life as it is unavoidable. A struggle successfully overcame or endured empowers, educates, invigorates, and motivates a man to violently attack his next would-be struggle. Struggle is as necessary a principle for life as sparring is for a fighter.

In Hollywood movies a man that has the courage to fight when provoked is a heroic man. But in reality, the courage of a man to violently fight when oppressed or provoked, is simply a requirement of a man!

The ABC's of a Black Man's Principles

The courage to fight through adversity is absolutely the defining substance of each man's own character. Character is a man's sword — which may only be sharpened through adversity.

For this reason I believe that struggle should be embraced, accepted, and encouraged within the Black community (especially within its Black males and especially for their progression). A Black man enduring a struggle for a progressive purpose should be absolutely commended and not at all discouraged. Every man should take pride in attaching himself to a progressive struggle and fight against its restraints violently.

Fredrick Douglass is a man who I believe may exemplify the true meaning of the word struggle. In a society that defined him as a domestic animal, and documented him as property to buy, rent, inherit, or sell; Douglass dedicated his lifetime to the struggle against the unjust and demonic restrictions that present societal era may have bound him to. In his words, "If there is no struggle there can be no progress." And I agree totally! If any man is audacious enough to pursue any type of progress for himself — he will undoubtedly meet a resistance to struggle with. In the same sense, if Black men are to pursue any type of social progress as a collective group, they should undoubtedly expect and accept a struggle.

The ABC's of a Black Man's Principles

In today's society Black men have been discouraged in and for their struggles. I would simply like to encourage them in both. Black men should not only accept a struggle, but sustain an encouraged morale and positive attitude while enduring it.

America is themed as "the land of the free" — but Black men cannot accept the overall present state of Black American people as sufficiently free. Black America only makes up about 12 percent of the American population. But the terrible disparity is that Black American males make up more than 40 percent of the American prison population. This statistic is a huge conflict to any alleged, or presumed, freedom or equality. We are still well short of equality in America. We are still short of the freedom offered in American opportunity. We are still under constraint. We are still under restriction. We still face difficulties. And we are still under certain social oppression; therefore a struggle is still required for Black men to engage upon.

Any Black American male that does not acknowledge our struggle against the American Justice system is a naïve, selfish, uneducated, and uninformed gentlemen. Across the American region, more Black American males are incarcerated in American Prisons than they are enrolled in American college institutions. This disproportion is not America's accountability. The accountability for this disproportion falls solely upon Black American males. The accountability of the American legislative system is to suit and govern its residence. If we don't object and fight violently against the American statutes that are crippling our community, then whose responsibility is it to do such? If Black men aren't willing to struggle against the American Justice System, then we will continue to struggle with it. (A struggle we are violently losing!)

Any American veteran will tell you that freedom isn't free. Black men should take a patriotic ownership of the opportunity for freedoms here in America and strive for more tangible rights and privileges as a collective group socially, financially, professionally, institutionally, developmentally, and sustainably.

The opportunity for a greater quality of life for all Black Americans is available and attainable. I believe the struggle towards that realization and its actualization should be a mandatory agenda.

To struggle is not good — it is terrible, but it is absolutely the most essential principle in a progressive man's life. To struggle builds character — and character builds communities.

The ABC's of a Black Man's Principles

*"Your own resolution to succeed is more important
than any other." – Abraham Lincoln*

T is for Tough. - The adjective tough is defined as able to withstand great strain without tearing or breaking. This is an applicable principle to not only Black men but every man. Every Man should have some degree of toughness because every man at some point will be placed under some type of pressure or strain and he should be able to withstand. For as much as the world today promotes the tendering of men, I believe that a man's ability to respond under pressure and withstand strain is still the classic intangible that measures a man.

In measurement of Black men, everyone knows that Black men are tough. We have to be tough. Black men have proven throughout history their ability to withstand the strains and pressures of the world. We should own our toughness and proudly be identified by it. Toughness is a very important quality in a Black man's life. We should not only be encouraging it in our young Black men, but developing and enhancing it as well.

However, the development of toughness should not be limited to itself physically— but mentally as well. I want to encourage young Black men's tenacity both mentally and physically. Toughness isn't just necessary in a Black man physically — it is also a principle that is much more relative to a Black man's mentality. The basis of Black progression was built upon struggle. When Black men cease to struggle we cease to progress. If we can encourage our young Black youth towards a mental toughness — the breakthroughs in the Black community's progression will be spectacular.

But everyone knows that "Tough — just *ain't* enough." A solid togetherness is also needed. I truly believe that the toughness of a Black community is best represented by its unison. A collective strength is always stronger then each of that same collection singularly.

In the 2011 movie, Planet of the Apes "Caesar," the main chimpanzee character, makes a point in sign language to a friendly orangutan. He parables that apes by themselves are weak by demonstratively snapping a single twig. He discards the broken twig, then bundles a group of twigs together, and bends them aggressively — but they do not break! "Apes together are strong," Caesar says, and I totally agreed.

I am far from the leader that Caesar was, and Black people are far from apes. But I also recognize that Black men and their community's greatest strength -lye in its togetherness. *"Tough ain't always enough,"* but together, it is definitely a tough agenda to bend.

A group of tough Black men, with a group of tough Black minds, is strengthened exponentially when gathered collectively. Imagine the potential of resources produced by such a unified force.

The ABC's of a Black Man's Principles

"When you know better, you do better."
- Maya Angelou

U is for Understanding - Depending on its form of noun or adjective — the word *understanding* may have several different meanings but each one is relative to a mental grasp or a comprehension. To be understanding in its adjective form is to be considerate, thoughtful, appreciative, and sympathetic. To have an understanding is to have a comprehension, intelligence or an implicit mutual agreement. A man's mental grasp of the things around him and how they work is a very essential principle. Maya Angelou once said, *"When you know better, you do better."*

This is why an understanding is imperative to a man's growth, progress, and success. As an example each and every newborn child is solely dependent upon his cognitive understanding before being capable of making even the smallest progressions. Before an infant is able to roll over or hold a bottle he is first dependent upon the development of his situational understanding. The infant must first process what he is experiencing before he can perform a proper response and navigate his motor skills. This principle continues throughout life. As our world expands and we become adults it is even more drastically important to develop our cognitive understanding of what it is we are experiencing. The better you understand your situation, the better your according response.

Chapter Eight

VWX's

"Our Destiny is largely in our hands"
- Fredrick Douglass

V is for Vigilant - To be vigilant means to be keenly watchful to detect danger and wary; ever awake and alert. This is a tough one. This is where I may even need help from a collective brotherhood on developing the balance per-spective of vigilance. It is not good to run around and be batman. It is definitely wrong to play police officer as George Zimmerman. But it is definitely not practical for an independent man to be solely dependent upon the police for his and his family's safety. Your safety and preventive precaution is upon yourself and your own responsibility. A Black man should not resolve to involve, the police for the mediation of every argument, threat, or confrontation.

This world is not a peaceful one and there are absolutely times when police presence is necessary and imperative. There also are times when altercation and even violence is necessary and unavoidable. My perspective is that a Black man should be deemed competent to resolve dangerous and threatening issues in accordance to the situation, using his own reasonable judgment. This however, is a process and a level that we would obviously need to work towards.

97

The ABC's of a Black Man's Principles

Police spend hundreds of academy hours in situation training to be the most practical resolve in emergency, violence, disturbance, and dispute. I believe that Black men should also be mandated to complete some type of equivalent training. It is very reasonable to assume that a Black male will be in some type of dispute or confrontation at some point in his life. Is it not also practical to prepare him with some type of comparative training to properly resolve that incident? Preparation is a pivotal key to life.

I am not saying that Black men as a group should take the place of police. I am saying that as a group of integrative men of principle — Black men, with preparative training and competent discernment, should look to police themselves.

"The LORD by wisdom founded the earth; By
understanding he established the heavens; by his
knowledge the depths were broken up and clouds
drop down the dew". - King Solomon; Proverbs 3: 19

W is for Wisdom - Wisdom is the ability to apply one's accumulation of knowledge, experience, understanding or common sense. It is your ability to discern or judge what is true and right. To have wisdom is to have a wise outlook, plan, or course of action. What else would you want in life other than a smart plan for it? King Solomon is considered to be the wisest man to have ever lived and the authority on wisdom. The book of Proverbs was written by King Solomon and is completely dedicated to the wisdom in seeking wisdom.

King Solomon writes thoroughly and poetically of the benefits, the value, the imperativeness, the securities, the excellence, and the way of wisdom. If you have never read the book of Proverbs than it would be wise of you to do such. If you have read the book of Proverbs, than you know how wise a person may feel just to recite from it. Wisdom is one of the core essentials in life. Each man should be looking to grow in his own accumulation of knowledge, experience, and overall understanding. Life as a dumb or foolish man (as Solomon would say) isn't the way God intended for Black men to live.

Ignorance is a choice of lazy, sluggardly, and evil men. The progressive growth of wisdom and understanding — should be the only acceptable way for young Black men to proceed through their lifetime. The necessity for the accumulation of knowledge and experience in practical disciplines such as business, banking, real- estate, and development is approaching a critical urgency for the Black community. It is extremely imperative to the future climate of Black communities for Black men to begin to consciously grow themselves in both Godly and worldly wisdom. If the Black community is to maintain, and self-sustain, it must first *gain* the wisdom necessary for those objectives. "Wise people store up knowledge, but the mouth of the foolish is near destruction."- Proverbs 10: 14

The ABC's of a Black Man's Principles

"In fact, once he is motivated no one can change
more completely than the man who has been at the
bottom. I call myself the best example of that."
-Malcolm X

X **is for Malcolm X -** Many of us value Malcolm and admire him as an icon, but never look into the values and principles that he represented as a man. His example of life is an example of stern principles, commitment, and progressive ideals. I think that Malcolm's message and example, aside of Martin's, is still the most relevant to the progression of Black community to this day.

When I was eleven years old I was hospitalized with a severe eye infection. I was taken to San Bernardino Community Hospital's Pediatrics and stayed an entire week. I was really sad and uncomfortable being away from home. To make me more comfortable, the next day, my grandmother brought me a bag of orange slices and my mother brought my Malcolm X painting from home to hang.

One of the nurses, a Black male, thought it was cool, but asked me appropriately what did Malcolm X stand for? Being immature and having only watched the movie I answered assertively, "Power baby." The nurse laughed, shook his head, and told me to keep thinking about that answer and walked out. I never saw him again, but I never ever forgot that question and how ignorant I felt blurting out so confidently what I (and many others as well) truly interpreted the "symbol of Malcolm X" to be. I never forgot that instant and I never forgot that question. It is true that Malcolm may have represented and now symbolizes many different things, including power. But what did Malcolm X stand for? The answer is change. Malcolm X stood up for change! But not just any type of change – a progressive change! Malcolm stood up for the progressive change within oneself, and the American system – but especially for Black people.

His audacious speeches and interviews were all based upon his ideals of change for, and within, the Black community. Malcolm's message was that Black people (starting with Black men) should take the audacious steps to build themselves as a self-sufficient community. A self-sufficient community with its own business, its own banks, its own governing, and its own real estate. Malcolm's message was for Black's to take upon themselves and initiate the necessary changes to empower themselves with the ability to sustain independently.

I'd like nothing more of my life than to revive this message that was killed with my God-Father Malcolm.

The ABC's of a Black Man's Principles

It is such a deep, scandalous, and ironic shame that such a great leader and man was killed by the very people that he committed his life to, and would have died to progress. Not only did Black men kill Malcolm, Black men are letting his message die.

Black men should never forget Malcolm, his example of a principled man, and his message for the progressive change toward self sufficiency for Black people. Each Black man should equally commit himself to the enthusiasm and audacity that Malcolm had for such a purpose.

I feel Malcolm's death to be as equal of an emasculation of a Godly chosen leader's message, deliverance, and agenda as if Moses had been killed by three Israelites upon his return to Egypt. (Think of where that would have left Israel. Still in Egypt right?)

As Jesus sacrificed his life and died for all people, Malcolm died for just one. Black men should never forget Malcolm and what he stood for. He stood for change, he stood for us. He stood for the change in us. You should too.

"I'm for truth, not matter who tells it. I'm for justice, no matter who it is for or against. I'm a human being, first and foremost, and as such I'm for whoever and whatever benefits humanity as a whole."

–Malcolm

Chapter Nine

Y&Z

The ABC's of a Black Man's Principles

Y is for Yielding –This one word may yield relevant principles in two quite different sense. To yield means to both produce and to grant allowance; to concede.

To yield as a producing principle is simple and direct in its effect. I think that each man is a yield of his own principles. A man's ultimate quality of life will depend directly upon the ultimate quality of his principles; or his lack thereof. A farmer yields exceptional crop or harvest from his dedication to exceptional sows. This is a direct effect. A man's principles and the quality of his life is the direct effect of the principle of yield.

"All men make mistakes, but a good man
yields when he knows his course is wrong, and
repairs the evil. The only crime is pride" –
Sophocles, Antigone

To yield in its conceding sense is more of a conscious effort. To yield in a conceding sense is a very powerful ideal. To me it means to give up ones selfish sense of entitlement. As an example, think of the big yellow yield sign in traffic. When approaching this big yellow sign you technically have the right away, but sometimes you may need to consider others and slow down! A yielding mentality is a considerate consciousness to share the right of way with others.

The Bible shares an example of two brothers, Esau and Jacob that were quite different. In this story the aggressive attitude of the eldest, and his inclination toward immediate gratification, causes him to sell his birth rights to the younger brother Jacob. The story goes on to many other relevant points such as "the first shall be last" and "the greater will serve the lesser," but my point is this...

Black men need to be cautious of some of our same aggressive tendencies and arrogance that caused Esau to lose his birth right. A belligerent attitude gets a man nowhere in life. Nobody owes a Black man anything. We are the most struggled, disenfranchised, and oppressed people to ever live. But, the progresses of our previous generations grant us the greatest opportunity to achieve equality that we may ever have and have had. In the present state of Black we do not have equality with our White, Asian, Latino, or even African brothers, but we do have the opportunity to realize such. The responsibility to capitalize and seize such favorable opportunity is our own.

With such in mind, a yielding mentally (and personality) is necessary and essential for a successful integration into relations with other races and demographics. To me, a yield is a relative cousin of

patience, reserve, and humility. Sometimes you have to give up ground

to gain ground. Sprinters take a pivotal step back to propel them forward.

Black men need to exercise a yield to the present superiority and

advancements of other races and learn to mimic and produce these same

successes for themselves. Pride and entitlement can cripple the opport-

unity for progressive growth. In such an urgent state for progressive

opportunity — Black men simply don't have the time to waste tending (or

pretending) to the self inflicted ails their pride and ignorance may have

caused them.

Black men are often considered as threats because of the strength

and fight in them. As I've indicated in earlier chapters, these are import-

ant elements in the make-up of a Black man. But it is also imperative that

we learn to reserve that strength, keep calm, and yield to other races the

right of way in our crossings, and learn to co-exist more peacefully and

productively. Our success and progress is our own responsibility and it is

highly dependent upon a cautious yield in our operative direction.

As a relevant side note; these crossings would be less frequent

and less sensitive if Black men established their own national structure

and didn't have to borrow so heavily as a dependent from our WA&L
brothers.

"Zeal is a volcano..." - Khaliil Gibran

Z is for Zeal - Zeal is the energetic and unflagging enthusiasm for a cause or idea. A zealous initiative can overcome any predicament. Faith is everything. You have to zealously believe in yourself and your cause for your community. A genuine zeal is contagious. If Black men enthusiastically believe that the enrichment of the Black community is a necessity — the rest of the world will too! We have to become adamant about our agenda. We have to become zealous about the work necessary in completing that agenda. Zeal is a great principle to top off one's complete self. It's also a great principle to wrap up this short book. A genuine zeal is the absolute cherry on top of all the principles. If Black men are to relay to the next generation this solid group of foundational principles and characteristics — an enthusiastic zeal is imperative.

Zeal is the closing sale of the entire collective group of principles. Why would a young boy want to work hard and long to obtain these essential principles, if no one has shown him their practical benefit? Black men have to possess a zeal for the principles that they build themselves upon. Each man can be his own strong individual based upon his application to the foundational principles zealously instilled within him by a strong Black community. We don't want to pass life's essentials on to our young generation passively. No, we want to pass our zealous beliefs onto our young Black men zealously!

A genuine zeal is contagious. And I zealously believe with all my heart that each of the principles contained in this book, are a necessary epidemic within the Black community.

Closing Word

A wise mentor of mine Mr. Melvin Ruffin once told me as I cut his hair, "Knowledge isn't power, workable knowledge is power!" Just as the Bible, the powerful lessons do not yield benefit without practical applications. So I thank you for your reading,but I now ask you to look for the applications of these readings and better yourself.

Progressive change and personal growth is the whole purpose! Keep reading, seeking God and growing. Take care, take time, and take all of God's blessings. Peace!

Acknowledgements

Thank you, heavenly father Yahweh for blessing me with such a voice to express myself literally. Thank you for developing that voice that I may praise you with it. You alone know my struggles with life and reverence. Thank you for your love and direction. In your son's name guide me further still.

Thank you, Yeshua for claiming my salvation from the prison of my sin and for being my witness to your father that I am of you and your likeness. I am you. I am your brother. I am your friend. Thanks for showing me such.

Thank you to those that have listened to my literary voice and encouraged its growth. Especially my Cynthia who has read every book idea, paper, blog, letter, note, and text message that I've ever wrote. I love you, appreciate you, and thank you twice.

Thank you to my Unc James Howard. Everything you have been for our family has been unappreciated and unacknowledged. I Love you and respect you.

Thank you to my Uncle David. Your words "don't limit yourself," have stuck with me and motivated me to be audacious and challenge myself.

Thank you to Mike Duran for blowing on my small flame with such a practical perspective of published writing and how cool it was.

I want to especially thank wonder woman, Mrs. Jo Scott-Coe. All my literary talent could never express what you've inspired in me to chase after your example.

And to my son. Cliché is to say that everything I do is for you, but more realistically, I want to impress you. I want you to be proud of me as if I was your son. As I write this I cry. You are the strongest emotion I have ever had. I just want to be worthy of you to come from me. Thanks for being my friend. Thanks for loving me for the crazy man that I am. Thanks for accepting me as your dad. You are such a motivation towards the positivity in me. I love you along with your mother as a family and I thank you.

Thanks lastly to myself. I'm very proud and impressed at the initiative and dedication that you've grown to and commend you for all the shit that you've grown through. I'm so sorry about your mother and what she did to you. I've witnessed you be your own motivation, your own educator, and your own encouragement as a child and adolescent. I commend your fortitude, respect your internal and external struggles, and love the fruition of you as a man. I pray my God bless you through your beautiful spirit. This book and everything I've ever written or do is truly for you. Stay you and keep going.

Dedication

To Wife Cynthia and my son Na'Sham Anthony.

To "Weebie"Juventino Montes "Jay R" and to my sister Tina.

To all those deceased whose memory weighs heavy upon my heart: Uncle Louis, Harold James, Ted James, Ernest Howard Sr., Robby and Annie Anderson, Marinell Ludd, Arthur Ludd, Louise Lewis, Eric Castaneda, Damian Liggins, John Beaudis, Jonathan Ordonez, "LR3,"Jonnie Van Dusen, and especially to my tia Gina, Brandon Harris, Laurenda Anne and Joy Wesley.

To my auntie Jocelyn. To my cousin "Bo."

To all my cousins and youth who may have looked to me as an example. To my God and to his will. To myself and my son. To young Black men and young Black authors. And again to myself and God.

I love this quote from Raquel Gordon, these are her words:

We're always talking about how broken black men are, but perhaps we should be focused on the rebuilding rather than the demolition.

The media is with the demolition crew. But as a black community, we need to be with the architects and the builders.

It's really up to us as a community to unite and build our Black men up regardless of what's in the media.
~Raquel Gordon

The ABC's of a Black Man's Principles

10 Quick Steps to Good Character

1. Love your God above all others, imprint His words on your heart, and let Him shape you into His image.

2. Learn to love and respect yourself so you can understand how to love and respect others and the environment.

3. Periodically assess your character in areas of self-discipline, trustworthiness, respectability, reliability, and dependability, and address your character flaws.

4. Be open to correction and don't be afraid to offer correction.

5. Take your education seriously, work towards a graduate degree, and create a plan for the foundation of your future.

6. Build a career based on honest business principles, strive towards leadership positions, and reach back for others on your way to the top.

7. Choose wisely and be responsible for the consequences of your actions.

8. Learn to be socially responsible and family oriented.

9. Learn to be financially responsible such that you provide for your family and give back to your community.

10. Appoint leaders and mentors who value and promote these principles as an example to others in the community.

"If you have built castles in the air, your work need not be lost this is where they should be, now put the foundation under them." -Henry David Thoreau

Thank You sincerely for your reading.
For further interest in my writing visit TheGritz.wordpress.com
Inquiries on appearances, booking, scheduled events, correspondence,
comments, or questions:
MarkAnthonyHoward00@gmail.com

MARK ANTHONY HOWARD
"THE GRITZ"

The ABC's of a Black Man's Principles

Made in the USA
Middletown, DE
16 March 2022

62707523R00068